Table Of Contents

Understanding the Basics of Email Automation 2
Benefits of Using Python for Email Automation 2
Overview of the smtplib and email Libraries 2
Chapter 2: Automating Weekly Email Newsletters 2
Setting Up a Python Script for Weekly Newsletter Creation 2
Sending Automated Newsletters Using smtplib 2
Customizing Newsletter Templates for Business Use 2
Chapter 3: Creating Python Scripts for Daily Sales Reports 2
Generating Daily Sales Reports with Python 2
Automating Email Delivery of Sales Reports 2
Implementing Data Visualization in Sales Reports 2
Chapter 4: Automating Monthly Progress Reports 2
Building a Python Script for Monthly Progress Reports 2
Sending Progress Reports to Team Members via Email 2
Analyzing and Tracking Progress Metrics in Reports 2
Chapter 5: Sending Personalized Birthday Emails to Clients 2
Creating a Python Script for Personalized Birthday Emails............ 2
Customizing Birthday Email Templates 2
Automating Birthday Email Delivery 2
Chapter 6: Automating Monthly Financial Reports 2
Generating Financial Reports with Python 2
Sending Financial Reports to Stakeholders via Email 2
Analyzing Financial Data and Trends in Reports 2
Chapter 7: Setting Up Reminders for Upcoming Deadlines 2
Building a Python Script for Automated Reminders 2
Sending Deadline Reminders via Email 2
Customizing Reminder Settings for Business Needs 2
Chapter 8: Automating Daily Weather Updates 2
Fetching Weather Data with Python 2
Sending Weather Updates via Email 2

- Customizing Weather Report Formats 2
- Chapter 9: Automating Weekly Project Status Reports 2
  - Creating Project Status Reports with Python 2
  - Sending Reports to Project Managers via Email 2
  - Tracking Project Progress and Milestones 2
- Chapter 10: Sending Event Reminders to Attendees 2
  - Building a Python Script for Event Reminders 2
  - Customizing Event Reminder Templates 2
  - Automating Reminder Delivery for Events 2
- Chapter 11: Setting Up Notifications for Website Uptime Monitoring
  2
  - Monitoring Website Uptime with Python 2
  - Sending Notifications for Website Downtime via Email 2
  - Customizing Monitoring Settings for Website Performance 2
- Chapter 12: Conclusion and Next Steps 2
  - Recap of Email Automation Strategies with Python 2
  - Tips for Enhancing Email Automation Efforts 2
  - Resources for Further Learning and Development 2
- Chapter 1: Introduction to Email Automation with Python 1

Python: Empowering the World through Simplicity and Versatility Introduction Python

Python is a general-purpose, high-level programming language 91

Python is an example of a general-purpose 93

Mastering Selection Statements in Python 95

Enhancing Python with Artificial Intelligence 99

Photograph credits go out 2 Designrr https://www.designrr.io 103

Chapter 1: Introduction to Email Automation with Python

Understanding the Basics of Email Automation

Email automation has become an essential tool for businesses looking to streamline their communication processes and increase efficiency. By utilizing Python scripts, businesses can automate the sending of various types of emails, such as weekly newsletters, daily sales reports, monthly progress reports, personalized birthday emails, and more. In this subchapter, we will delve into the basics of email automation using Python and explore how businesses can leverage this powerful tool to enhance their communication strategies.

Automating weekly email newsletters using the smtplib and email libraries is a common practice among businesses looking to engage with their audience on a regular basis. By creating a Python script that pulls content from a designated source and sends it out to subscribers automatically, businesses can save time and ensure that their newsletters are consistently delivered on schedule.

Creating a Python script to send automated daily sales reports via email is another valuable application of email automation for businesses. By setting up a script that retrieves sales data from a database or CRM system and formats it into a report, businesses can ensure that key stakeholders receive timely updates on sales performance without manual intervention.

Using Python to automate sending monthly progress reports to team members is a great way for businesses to keep their employees informed and motivated. By setting up a script that compiles project milestones, KPIs, and other relevant data into a monthly report and sends it out to team members automatically, businesses can foster transparency and accountability within their organization.

Building a script to send personalized birthday emails to clients using Python is a thoughtful way for businesses to strengthen relationships with their customers. By creating a script that pulls client birthdays from a database and sends out personalized birthday greetings and offers, businesses can show their clients that they value their patronage and care about their individual needs.

Automating the sending of monthly financial reports to stakeholders with Python is a crucial task for businesses looking to keep investors, board members, and other key stakeholders informed about their financial performance. By setting up a script that generates financial reports from accounting software and sends them out via email, businesses can ensure that stakeholders have access to timely and accurate financial information.

Benefits of Using Python for Email Automation

Email automation has become an essential tool for businesses looking to streamline their communication processes and improve efficiency. Python, a versatile and powerful programming language, offers a range of benefits for automating email tasks. In this subchapter, we will explore the various advantages of using Python for email automation in a business setting.

One of the key benefits of using Python for email automation is its simplicity and ease of use. Python's clean and readable syntax makes it easy for even novice programmers to quickly create scripts for sending automated emails. This can be particularly useful for businesses that do not have dedicated IT resources or programming expertise, allowing them to automate email tasks with minimal effort.

Another advantage of using Python for email automation is its flexibility and versatility. Python offers a wide range of libraries and modules specifically designed for working with emails, such as smtplib and email. These libraries provide a wealth of functionality for sending, receiving, and managing emails, making it easy to customize and automate email processes to suit the specific needs of a business.

Python's ability to interact with external APIs and web services also makes it an ideal choice for automating email tasks. For example, businesses can use Python to pull data from a CRM system or online database and use this information to personalize and target email campaigns. This can help businesses to improve the effectiveness of their email marketing efforts and drive better results.

In addition to its technical capabilities, Python's community support and extensive documentation make it a valuable resource for businesses looking to implement email automation. The Python community is active and vibrant, with a wealth of resources and tutorials available to help businesses get started with email automation. This can be particularly beneficial for businesses looking to quickly implement email automation solutions without the need for extensive training or support.

Overall, using Python for email automation offers a range of benefits for businesses of all sizes and industries. Whether automating weekly newsletters, sending daily sales reports, or personalized birthday emails, Python provides a powerful and flexible platform for streamlining email communication processes and improving efficiency. By harnessing the power of Python for email automation, businesses can save time, reduce manual effort, and enhance the effectiveness of their email marketing and communication strategies.

Overview of the smtplib and email Libraries

In this subchapter, we will delve into the powerful smtplib and email libraries in Python that allow businesses to efficiently automate their email communications. These libraries offer a wide range of functionalities that can streamline the process of sending out newsletters, reports, reminders, and notifications to various stakeholders.

Automating weekly email newsletters using the smtplib and email libraries can save businesses valuable time and resources. With Python scripts, businesses can schedule newsletters to be sent out at a specific time each week, ensuring that their audience receives timely updates and information. This automation process eliminates the need for manual intervention, leading to a more efficient and effective communication strategy.

Creating a Python script to send automated daily sales reports via email is another valuable use case for the smtplib and email libraries. By automating the process of generating and sending sales reports, businesses can ensure that key stakeholders are kept informed of daily performance metrics. This level of automation not only saves time but also ensures that reports are consistently delivered in a timely manner.

Using Python to automate sending monthly progress reports to team members is essential for keeping everyone on the same page. By leveraging the smtplib and email libraries, businesses can set up scripts to automatically generate and distribute progress reports at the end of each month. This streamlined approach to communication fosters transparency and accountability within the team.

Building a script to send personalized birthday emails to clients using Python can help businesses strengthen client relationships and foster loyalty. By automating the process of sending personalized birthday greetings, businesses can show their clients that they are valued and appreciated. The smtplib and email libraries make it easy to customize and personalize these emails, creating a memorable experience for clients.

In conclusion, the smtplib and email libraries in Python offer businesses a powerful toolkit for automating their email communications. From sending out weekly newsletters to personalized birthday emails, these libraries enable businesses to streamline their communication processes and improve efficiency. By leveraging the capabilities of Python, businesses can save time, resources, and effort while maintaining a high level of professionalism in their email communications.

Chapter 2: Automating Weekly Email Newsletters

Setting Up a Python Script for Weekly Newsletter Creation

Automating weekly email newsletters using the smtplib and email libraries can save businesses valuable time and effort. By setting up a Python script to handle the creation and sending of newsletters, businesses can ensure that their subscribers receive regular updates and information in a timely manner. This subchapter will guide businesses through the process of setting up a Python script for weekly newsletter creation, providing step-by-step instructions and best practices for efficient email automation.

Creating a Python script to send automated daily sales reports via email is a valuable tool for businesses looking to streamline their reporting processes. By automating the generation and sending of daily sales reports, businesses can ensure that key stakeholders are kept informed of sales performance on a regular basis. This subchapter will outline the necessary steps for setting up a Python script to handle the automated creation and distribution of daily sales reports via email.

Using Python to automate sending monthly progress reports to team members can help businesses keep their teams informed and motivated. By setting up a Python script to generate and send monthly progress reports, businesses can ensure that team members are aware of project milestones, goals, and accomplishments. This subchapter will provide businesses with the guidance they need to create a Python script for automating the sending of monthly progress reports to team members.

Building a script to send personalized birthday emails to clients using Python is a thoughtful way for businesses to engage with their customers. By automating the process of sending personalized birthday emails, businesses can strengthen customer relationships and demonstrate their commitment to customer satisfaction. This subchapter will walk businesses through the process of setting up a Python script for sending personalized birthday emails to clients.

Automating the sending of monthly financial reports to stakeholders with Python can help businesses streamline their financial reporting processes. By setting up a Python script to handle the generation and distribution of monthly financial reports, businesses can ensure that stakeholders receive accurate and timely financial information. This subchapter will provide businesses with the tools and techniques they need to create a Python script for automating the sending of monthly financial reports to stakeholders.

Sending Automated Newsletters Using smtplib

In the world of business, staying connected with clients, team members, and stakeholders is crucial. One way to keep everyone informed and engaged is through automated newsletters sent via email. By using the smtplib library in Python, businesses can streamline the process of sending out weekly updates, sales reports, progress reports, birthday greetings, financial reports, reminders, and more.

The smtplib library in Python allows businesses to automate the process of sending emails, making it easier to keep everyone in the loop. By creating a Python script that utilizes the smtplib library, businesses can schedule and send out daily, weekly, monthly, or even yearly newsletters with ease. This not only saves time but also ensures that important information is consistently delivered to the right people at the right time.

For businesses looking to automate the sending of daily sales reports via email, the smtplib library is a valuable tool. By creating a Python script that pulls data from sales databases or CRM systems and formats it into a report, businesses can use the smtplib library to send these reports to key stakeholders automatically. This ensures that sales performance is communicated in a timely manner and helps keep everyone on the same page.

In addition to sales reports, businesses can also use the smtplib library to automate the sending of monthly progress reports to team members. By setting up a Python script that pulls data from project management tools and formats it into a digestible report, businesses can use the smtplib library to send these reports to team members on a regular basis. This helps keep everyone informed of project progress and fosters collaboration within the team.

Overall, the smtplib library in Python is a powerful tool for businesses looking to streamline their email automation processes. Whether it's sending birthday greetings to clients, financial reports to stakeholders, reminders for upcoming deadlines, or event notifications to attendees, the smtplib library can help businesses automate these tasks and ensure that important information is delivered in a timely manner. By leveraging the smtplib library, businesses can save time, improve communication, and enhance overall efficiency in their email automation efforts.

Customizing Newsletter Templates for Business Use

In the world of business, communication is key. One of the most effective ways to keep in touch with clients, stakeholders, and team members is through email newsletters. These newsletters can provide updates on company progress, sales reports, project status, event reminders, and more. However, manually creating and sending these emails can be time-consuming and inefficient. That's where Python automation comes in.

Automating weekly email newsletters using the smtplib and email libraries is a game-changer for businesses looking to streamline their communication processes. By creating a Python script to generate and send out newsletters on a regular basis, businesses can save time and ensure consistency in their messaging. With just a few lines of code, businesses can customize newsletter templates to include company branding, relevant content, and personalized greetings.

Creating a Python script to send automated daily sales reports via email is another way to leverage automation for business success. By pulling data from sales databases or CRM systems, businesses can generate reports in real-time and send them to key stakeholders with ease. This not only saves time but also ensures that sales data is accurate and up-to-date.

Using Python to automate sending monthly progress reports to team members is a great way to keep everyone on the same page. By scheduling automated emails with progress updates, businesses can improve communication and collaboration within their teams. This can be especially useful for remote teams or large organizations where keeping everyone informed can be a challenge.

Building a script to send personalized birthday emails to clients using Python is a thoughtful way to show appreciation and build customer loyalty. By automating the process of sending birthday greetings, businesses can create a more personal connection with their clients. This small gesture can go a long way in strengthening relationships and increasing customer satisfaction.

Chapter 3: Creating Python Scripts for Daily Sales Reports

Generating Daily Sales Reports with Python

In the modern business world, automation plays a crucial role in streamlining processes and increasing efficiency. One area where automation can greatly benefit businesses is in the generation of daily sales reports. With Python, a powerful programming language known for its simplicity and versatility, businesses can easily create scripts to automate the generation and sending of daily sales reports via email.

By utilizing Python's smtplib and email libraries, businesses can create a Python script that pulls data from their sales database and formats it into a concise daily sales report. This report can then be automatically sent to designated recipients, ensuring that key stakeholders are kept informed of daily sales performance without any manual intervention.

Not only does automating daily sales reports save time and reduce the risk of human error, but it also allows businesses to stay proactive and responsive to market trends. With timely and accurate sales data at their fingertips, businesses can make informed decisions and adjust their strategies as needed to maximize revenue and profitability.

Furthermore, Python can be used to automate the sending of monthly progress reports to team members, personalized birthday emails to clients, monthly financial reports to stakeholders, and much more. The possibilities for automation with Python are endless, offering businesses the opportunity to streamline their operations and improve communication with stakeholders.

In conclusion, by harnessing the power of Python for automating daily sales reports and other email communications, businesses can increase their efficiency, improve decision-making, and ultimately drive growth and success. Whether it's sending weather updates, project status reports, event reminders, or website uptime notifications, Python offers a versatile and user-friendly solution for automating email communications in any business setting.

Automating Email Delivery of Sales Reports

In today's fast-paced business world, staying on top of sales reports and progress updates is essential for success. One way to streamline this process is by automating the delivery of these reports via email. By using Python, businesses can create scripts that will send out these reports on a regular basis, saving time and ensuring that important information is always delivered in a timely manner.

One common use case for automating email delivery of sales reports is sending out weekly newsletters to clients and stakeholders. By using the smtplib and email libraries in Python, businesses can create a script that pulls in the latest sales data and automatically sends it out in a visually appealing format. This not only saves time for employees who would otherwise have to manually compile and send out these reports, but also ensures that everyone is kept up to date on the latest sales figures.

Another useful application of automating email delivery of sales reports is sending out daily updates to team members. By creating a Python script that pulls in the latest sales data and automatically sends it out to the relevant team members, businesses can ensure that everyone is on the same page and working towards the same goals. This can help improve communication and collaboration within the team, leading to better overall performance and results.

In addition to sending out sales reports, businesses can also use Python to automate the delivery of monthly progress reports to team members. By creating a script that pulls in data from various sources and compiles it into a comprehensive progress report, businesses can ensure that everyone is aware of the current status of projects and initiatives. This can help improve accountability and transparency within the organization, leading to more informed decision-making and better overall performance.

Overall, automating the delivery of sales reports and progress updates via email can help businesses save time, improve communication, and ensure that important information is always delivered in a timely manner. By using Python to create scripts that automate these processes, businesses can streamline their operations and focus on what really matters – growing their business and achieving their goals.

Implementing Data Visualization in Sales Reports

Data visualization is a powerful tool that can greatly enhance the effectiveness of sales reports. By presenting sales data in a visual format, businesses can quickly and easily identify trends, patterns, and outliers that might otherwise go unnoticed. In this subchapter, we will explore how to implement data visualization techniques in sales reports using Python.

One of the key benefits of using data visualization in sales reports is that it allows businesses to communicate complex information in a simple and easy-to-understand way. By creating charts, graphs, and other visualizations, businesses can make it easier for stakeholders to quickly grasp important sales metrics such as revenue, profit margins, and sales growth over time.

To implement data visualization in sales reports, businesses can use Python libraries such as Matplotlib and Seaborn. These libraries provide a wide range of tools for creating visually appealing charts and graphs that can be easily integrated into sales reports. By using these libraries, businesses can customize the look and feel of their visualizations to match their brand aesthetic and communicate information effectively.

In addition to creating static visualizations, businesses can also use Python to create interactive sales dashboards that allow stakeholders to explore sales data in real-time. By building interactive dashboards, businesses can empower stakeholders to drill down into sales data, filter information based on specific criteria, and gain deeper insights into sales performance.

Overall, implementing data visualization in sales reports using Python can help businesses improve decision-making, drive sales growth, and enhance overall business performance. By leveraging the power of data visualization, businesses can transform their sales reports into valuable tools for driving success in today's competitive business environment.

Chapter 4: Automating Monthly Progress Reports

Building a Python Script for Monthly Progress Reports

In this subchapter, we will explore the process of building a Python script for generating and sending monthly progress reports. Monthly progress reports are essential for businesses to track their performance, set goals for the upcoming month, and communicate key achievements to team members and stakeholders. By automating this process with Python, businesses can save time and ensure that reports are consistently delivered on time.

To begin, we will outline the key components of a monthly progress report, including metrics such as sales figures, project milestones, and key performance indicators. By identifying the specific data points that need to be included in the report, businesses can ensure that the information is accurate and relevant to the intended audience. Once the data points have been determined, we can move on to creating a Python script that will collect this data from various sources and compile it into a cohesive report.

Next, we will discuss how to use Python to format the report in a visually appealing way. This may involve using libraries such as Pandas and Matplotlib to create tables, charts, and graphs that effectively communicate the data. By presenting the information in a clear and concise manner, businesses can ensure that team members and stakeholders can easily digest and interpret the report.

After the report has been compiled and formatted, we will demonstrate how to use Python to automate the process of sending it via email. By utilizing the smtplib and email libraries, businesses can set up a script that will automatically generate the report, attach it to an email, and send it to the designated recipients. This automation not only saves time but also reduces the risk of human error in the reporting process.

In conclusion, building a Python script for monthly progress reports can greatly streamline the reporting process for businesses of all sizes. By automating the collection, formatting, and distribution of data, businesses can ensure that their team members and stakeholders are kept informed of key developments on a regular basis. With the right tools and techniques, businesses can leverage the power of Python to create efficient and effective reporting systems that support their overall success.

Sending Progress Reports to Team Members via Email

Sending progress reports to team members via email is an essential task for many businesses. By automating this process using Python, you can save time and ensure that everyone stays informed about the progress of projects and tasks. In this subchapter, we will explore how to use Python to send progress reports to team members via email.

One way to automate the sending of progress reports is to create a Python script that pulls data from your project management system or other sources and formats it into a report. You can then use the smtplib and email libraries in Python to send this report as an email attachment to team members. This approach allows you to customize the content of the report and ensure that it is delivered in a consistent format each time.

Another option is to use Python to generate personalized progress reports for each team member. By pulling data from individual project tasks or milestones, you can create reports that are tailored to each team member's role and responsibilities. This personalized approach can help team members stay engaged and motivated, as they will receive information that is directly relevant to their work.

In addition to sending progress reports on a regular basis, you can also use Python to automate the sending of reminders and notifications to team members. For example, you can set up automated reminders for upcoming deadlines or send notifications about changes to project timelines. By using Python to handle these routine communications, you can free up time for more strategic tasks and ensure that important information is always communicated in a timely manner.

Overall, automating the sending of progress reports to team members via email can help streamline communication within your organization and ensure that everyone is on the same page. Whether you are sending weekly project status updates, monthly progress reports, or personalized notifications, Python can help you automate these processes and save time for more important tasks. By following the tips and techniques outlined in this subchapter, you can efficiently use Python to keep your team informed and engaged.

Analyzing and Tracking Progress Metrics in Reports

Analyzing and tracking progress metrics in reports is an essential aspect of any business operation. By utilizing Python scripts and automation techniques, businesses can streamline their reporting processes and ensure that key stakeholders are consistently informed of important updates and developments. In this subchapter, we will explore various methods for automating the generation and distribution of reports using Python, with a focus on email newsletters, sales reports, progress reports, birthday emails, financial reports, reminders, weather updates, project status reports, event reminders, and website monitoring notifications.

Automating weekly email newsletters using the smtplib and email libraries is a powerful way to keep customers and clients engaged with your business. By creating a Python script that pulls in relevant content and automatically sends it out on a regular basis, businesses can save time and effort while maintaining a consistent communication strategy. This approach is especially useful for businesses that rely on email marketing to drive sales and engage with their audience.

Creating a Python script to send automated daily sales reports via email can help businesses track their performance and identify trends in real-time. By pulling data from a sales database or CRM system, businesses can generate personalized reports that provide insights into key metrics such as revenue, conversion rates, and customer acquisition. These reports can be automatically sent out to sales teams, managers, and other stakeholders, ensuring that everyone is on the same page and working towards common goals.

Using Python to automate sending monthly progress reports to team members is a great way to keep everyone informed of project developments and milestones. By pulling data from project management tools or databases, businesses can create detailed reports that highlight progress, challenges, and next steps. These reports can be automatically generated and sent out to team members, ensuring that everyone is aware of their responsibilities and deadlines.

Building a script to send personalized birthday emails to clients using Python is a thoughtful way to show appreciation and build customer loyalty. By integrating with a CRM system or customer database, businesses can create personalized email templates that are automatically sent out on each client's birthday. This personal touch can help businesses strengthen their relationships with clients and encourage repeat business.

Automating the sending of monthly financial reports to stakeholders with Python is a crucial task for businesses looking to maintain transparency and accountability. By pulling data from accounting software or financial databases, businesses can generate detailed reports that provide insights into revenue, expenses, and profitability. These reports can be automatically sent out to stakeholders, such as investors, board members, and executives, ensuring that everyone is informed of the company's financial health.

Chapter 5: Sending Personalized Birthday Emails to Clients

Creating a Python Script for Personalized Birthday Emails

In this subchapter, we will delve into the process of creating a Python script for personalized birthday emails. This is a fantastic way for businesses to show their clients that they care and appreciate them on their special day. By automating this process, you can ensure that no birthdays are missed and that each client receives a personalized message from your business.

To begin, you will need to make sure you have the necessary libraries installed in Python. The smtplib and email libraries are essential for sending emails programmatically. Once you have these libraries set up, you can start writing your script to send personalized birthday emails. You will need to gather the necessary information, such as the client's name and email address, as well as the message you want to send.

Next, you can use Python to format the email with the client's name and a personalized birthday message. This will make each email feel unique and special, enhancing the client's experience with your business. You can also set up your script to send these emails automatically on the client's birthday, saving you time and ensuring that no birthdays are overlooked.

By automating the process of sending personalized birthday emails, you can strengthen your relationships with clients and show them that you value their business. This small gesture can go a long way in building customer loyalty and increasing client satisfaction. With Python, you can streamline this process and make it easy to send personalized birthday emails to all your clients.

Overall, creating a Python script for personalized birthday emails is a simple yet effective way to enhance your business's communication with clients. By automating this process, you can ensure that each client receives a personalized message on their special day, strengthening your relationships and fostering customer loyalty. With the power of Python, you can easily set up this automated system and make sending personalized birthday emails a seamless part of your business operations.

Customizing Birthday Email Templates

One of the key aspects of email automation is personalization, and what better way to personalize your emails than by sending customized birthday greetings to your clients? In this subchapter, we will explore how to use Python to build a script that sends personalized birthday emails to clients automatically.

To begin, you will need to create an email template that includes placeholders for the recipient's name and birthday. Using Python's email library, you can easily load this template and replace the placeholders with the actual name and birthday of each client in your email list.

Next, you will need to set up a database or CSV file that contains the names and birthdays of your clients. By using Python to read this data and iterate through each client, you can dynamically generate and send personalized birthday emails to each recipient.

In order to ensure that your birthday emails are sent on time, you can schedule your Python script to run daily and check for any upcoming birthdays. By setting up a cron job or using a task scheduler, you can automate the sending of birthday emails without any manual intervention.

By customizing your birthday email templates with Python, you can show your clients that you care about them on their special day. This personal touch can help to strengthen your relationships with clients and increase customer loyalty, making it a valuable addition to your email automation strategy.

Automating Birthday Email Delivery

In the world of business, communication is key. Whether it's sending out weekly newsletters, daily sales reports, or monthly progress updates, staying in touch with clients, team members, and stakeholders is essential for success. With the power of Python, businesses can automate the process of sending out these important emails, saving time and ensuring that no message falls through the cracks.

One key area where Python automation can be incredibly useful is in the delivery of birthday emails. By building a script that pulls client birthdays from a database and sends out personalized birthday greetings, businesses can show their clients that they care and appreciate their business. This not only strengthens client relationships but also helps to build brand loyalty.

Another important task that can be automated using Python is the sending of monthly financial reports to stakeholders. By creating a script that generates these reports and automatically sends them out via email, businesses can ensure that stakeholders are kept informed and up-to-date on the financial health of the company. This can help to build trust and confidence in the business, leading to stronger partnerships and increased investment.

For project managers, automating the delivery of weekly project status reports can be a game-changer. By using Python to generate these reports and send them out on a regular basis, project managers can keep their teams informed and on track, leading to more efficient and successful project outcomes. This can help to streamline communication and collaboration within the team, ultimately leading to improved project performance.

In addition to these tasks, Python automation can also be used to send out daily weather updates, event reminders, and website uptime notifications. By setting up scripts to handle these routine tasks, businesses can free up valuable time and resources to focus on more important aspects of their operations. With the power of Python, businesses can streamline their email communication processes and ensure that important messages are delivered in a timely and efficient manner.

Chapter 6: Automating Monthly Financial Reports

Generating Financial Reports with Python

Sending Financial Reports to Stakeholders via Email

In today's fast-paced business world, staying on top of financial reports and communicating them effectively to stakeholders is crucial for success. One efficient way to do this is by automating the process of sending financial reports via email. This not only saves time and reduces human error but also ensures that stakeholders receive the information they need in a timely manner. In this subchapter, we will explore how businesses can leverage the power of Python to automate the sending of financial reports to stakeholders through email.

One key aspect of sending financial reports via email is ensuring that the information is accurate and up-to-date. By using Python scripts to automate this process, businesses can easily pull data from their financial systems and generate reports in real-time. This eliminates the need for manual intervention and ensures that stakeholders are receiving the most current information available.

Another benefit of automating the sending of financial reports via email is the ability to personalize the content for each stakeholder. By using Python to dynamically populate report templates with individualized data, businesses can tailor the information to meet the specific needs of each recipient. This not only enhances the overall user experience but also increases the impact of the communication.

Furthermore, automating the sending of financial reports via email allows businesses to set up recurring schedules for delivery. Whether it's sending weekly, monthly, or quarterly reports, Python scripts can be configured to automatically generate and send reports at predefined intervals. This ensures that stakeholders are consistently informed about the financial health of the business without any manual intervention.

Overall, leveraging Python for sending financial reports to stakeholders via email is a powerful way for businesses to streamline their communication processes and improve overall efficiency. By automating the generation, customization, and delivery of financial reports, businesses can ensure that stakeholders have access to the information they need, when they need it. This not only strengthens relationships with stakeholders but also positions businesses for continued success in an increasingly competitive market.

Analyzing Financial Data and Trends in Reports

In this subchapter, we will delve into the importance of analyzing financial data and trends in reports for all businesses. By automating the process of sending out weekly newsletters and reports using Python, businesses can save time and resources while keeping stakeholders informed and engaged. With the help of libraries like smtplib and email, businesses can easily create personalized and professional-looking emails that deliver key financial information in a timely manner.

One of the key benefits of using Python to automate the sending of daily sales reports via email is the ability to track and monitor sales performance in real-time. By setting up a Python script to gather and analyze sales data, businesses can quickly identify trends and make informed decisions to drive revenue growth. This automated process not only saves time but also ensures that stakeholders receive up-to-date information on a daily basis.

Similarly, using Python to automate the sending of monthly progress reports to team members can help improve communication and collaboration within an organization. By building a script that pulls data from various sources and compiles it into a comprehensive report, businesses can keep team members informed about project milestones, goals, and challenges. This automated process fosters transparency and accountability, leading to more efficient decision-making and project management.

Another valuable application of Python in business automation is the ability to send personalized birthday emails to clients. By setting up a script that triggers automated birthday greetings based on client data, businesses can strengthen relationships and enhance customer loyalty. This personalized touch not only shows appreciation but also helps businesses stay top of mind and differentiate themselves from competitors.

In addition to sending personalized birthday emails, businesses can also use Python to automate the sending of monthly financial reports to stakeholders. By building a script that generates and sends out financial reports on a regular basis, businesses can keep stakeholders informed about the company's financial health and performance. This automated process ensures that stakeholders have access to critical financial information in a timely manner, enabling them to make informed decisions and support the business's growth and success.

Chapter 7: Setting Up Reminders for Upcoming Deadlines

Building a Python Script for Automated Reminders

In the subchapter "Building a Python Script for Automated Reminders" in the book "Efficient Email Automation: A Guide to Using Python for Weekly Newsletters and Reports in Business", we will explore the various ways businesses can utilize Python scripting to streamline their communication processes. From automating weekly email newsletters to sending personalized birthday emails to clients, Python offers a wide range of possibilities for efficient email automation.

One popular use case for Python scripting in business is automating the sending of automated reminders for upcoming deadlines. By setting up a Python script to send reminders via email, businesses can ensure that team members stay on track and meet important project milestones. This not only helps to improve productivity but also reduces the risk of missing crucial deadlines.

Another common application of Python scripting in business is automating the sending of monthly progress reports to team members. By creating a Python script that generates and sends out progress reports automatically, businesses can save time and ensure that everyone is kept informed of the latest developments. This can help to improve communication within the team and ensure that everyone is on the same page.

Python scripting can also be used to automate the sending of personalized birthday emails to clients. By building a Python script that pulls in client data and generates personalized birthday messages, businesses can show their clients that they care and strengthen customer relationships. This personal touch can go a long way in building loyalty and trust with clients.

Furthermore, businesses can use Python scripting to automate the sending of monthly financial reports to stakeholders. By setting up a Python script that generates and sends out financial reports automatically, businesses can keep stakeholders informed of the company's financial performance without manual intervention. This can help to improve transparency and accountability within the organization.

Overall, Python scripting offers businesses a powerful tool for automating their email communication processes. From sending automated reminders for upcoming deadlines to generating personalized birthday emails for clients, Python can help businesses streamline their communication efforts and save time. By leveraging the capabilities of Python, businesses can improve efficiency, enhance communication, and strengthen relationships with clients and stakeholders.

Sending Deadline Reminders via Email

One of the key aspects of running a successful business is ensuring that all deadlines are met in a timely manner. However, with so many tasks and responsibilities to juggle, it can be easy for deadlines to slip through the cracks. This is where email automation comes in handy. By setting up automated email reminders for upcoming deadlines, businesses can ensure that no task is forgotten or left incomplete.

Automating deadline reminders using Python is a simple and efficient way to stay on top of important tasks. By utilizing the smtplib and email libraries, businesses can easily create a Python script that sends out reminder emails to team members as deadlines approach. This not only helps keep everyone on track, but also fosters a culture of accountability and responsibility within the organization.

Creating a Python script to send automated deadline reminders is a straightforward process. Businesses can customize the content of the email, including details about the upcoming deadline, any relevant information or instructions, and a gentle reminder to ensure that the task is completed on time. By scheduling these emails to be sent out at regular intervals leading up to the deadline, businesses can effectively keep everyone informed and motivated to meet their responsibilities.

Automated deadline reminders can be used for a variety of purposes within a business. Whether it's reminding team members about project milestones, sales targets, or upcoming events, Python can be utilized to streamline the process and ensure that important deadlines are never missed. By setting up automated reminders, businesses can improve efficiency, productivity, and overall performance.

In conclusion, sending deadline reminders via email using Python is a valuable tool for businesses looking to stay organized and on track. By automating this process, businesses can reduce the risk of missed deadlines, improve communication within the organization, and ultimately achieve greater success. With the power of Python and email automation, businesses can take control of their deadlines and ensure that tasks are completed in a timely manner.

Customizing Reminder Settings for Business Needs

In the world of business, efficient communication is key to success. One way to streamline communication processes is by automating email reminders using Python scripts. Customizing reminder settings for business needs allows for tailored and timely notifications to be sent to team members, clients, and stakeholders. Whether it's sending weekly project status reports, daily sales updates, or monthly progress reports, Python can help businesses stay organized and on track.

Automating weekly email newsletters using the smtplib and email libraries is a great way to keep customers and clients informed about upcoming events, promotions, and company news. By setting up a Python script to send automated reminders for upcoming deadlines through email, businesses can ensure that important tasks are completed on time. Additionally, using Python to automate the sending of monthly financial reports to stakeholders can save time and reduce the risk of human error in data entry.

Creating a Python script to send personalized birthday emails to clients is a thoughtful way to show appreciation and strengthen relationships. By setting up a Python script to send automated event reminders to attendees, businesses can ensure that everyone is informed and prepared for upcoming meetings, conferences, or webinars. Moreover, using Python to automate the sending of weekly project status reports to project managers can improve communication and collaboration within teams.

Building a script to send automated daily sales reports via email can help businesses track performance metrics and identify areas for improvement. Setting up a Python script to send automated notifications for website uptime monitoring via email ensures that technical issues are addressed promptly, minimizing downtime and potential losses. By customizing reminder settings for business needs, companies can leverage the power of Python to streamline communication processes and improve overall efficiency.

Chapter 8: Automating Daily Weather Updates

Fetching Weather Data with Python

In this subchapter, we will explore how to fetch weather data using Python to enhance your business automation processes. By incorporating weather data into your emails, you can provide valuable information to your recipients and tailor your messages based on current weather conditions.

To begin fetching weather data with Python, you will first need to choose a weather API to access real-time weather information. Popular options include OpenWeatherMap, Weather Underground, and AccuWeather. Once you have selected an API, you can use Python's requests library to make HTTP requests and retrieve weather data in JSON format.

Next, you will need to parse the JSON response to extract the relevant weather information, such as temperature, humidity, wind speed, and precipitation. You can use Python's built-in json module to easily parse the JSON data and extract the desired weather parameters.

After extracting the weather data, you can incorporate it into your email automation scripts to provide personalized weather updates to your recipients. For example, you can include the current temperature and weather conditions in your daily sales reports, monthly progress reports, or weekly project status updates to add value to your communications.

By fetching weather data with Python, you can create dynamic and engaging emails that are tailored to the recipient's location and current weather conditions. This level of personalization can help improve engagement and build stronger relationships with your audience, ultimately enhancing the effectiveness of your email automation efforts.

Sending Weather Updates via Email

Sending weather updates via email can be a useful tool for businesses looking to keep their clients, employees, or stakeholders informed about changing weather conditions that may impact their operations. By using Python to automate the process of sending weather updates, businesses can save time and ensure that important information is delivered in a timely manner.

To begin sending weather updates via email, businesses can utilize the smtplib and email libraries in Python to create a script that retrieves weather data from a reliable source, such as a weather API. By incorporating this data into an email template, businesses can customize the content of the weather updates to include relevant information such as current temperature, humidity, precipitation, and upcoming weather forecasts.

Creating a Python script to send automated weather updates via email can be particularly beneficial for businesses in industries that are sensitive to weather conditions, such as agriculture, construction, or event planning. By automating the process of sending weather updates, businesses can ensure that their stakeholders are well-informed and prepared for any potential disruptions that may arise due to inclement weather.

In addition to sending basic weather updates, businesses can also personalize their emails by including specific recommendations or tips for how recipients can prepare for upcoming weather events. For example, a construction company may include safety precautions for workers during extreme weather conditions, or a retail store may suggest promotions or products that are relevant to the current weather forecast.

Overall, automating the process of sending weather updates via email using Python can help businesses streamline their communication efforts, improve efficiency, and enhance their relationships with clients, employees, and stakeholders. By leveraging the power of Python to automate this task, businesses can ensure that important weather information is delivered promptly and accurately, ultimately contributing to their overall success and productivity.

Customizing Weather Report Formats

In this subchapter, we will explore the process of customizing weather report formats for your automated email updates. Weather reports can be a valuable addition to your weekly newsletters or daily updates, providing your audience with relevant and timely information. By customizing the format of these reports, you can ensure that they are clear, concise, and visually appealing to your readers.

One way to customize weather report formats is to include specific details that are relevant to your audience. For example, if you are sending weather updates to clients in different regions, you may want to include information about temperature, precipitation, and wind speed for each location. This can help your audience better understand the weather conditions in their area and plan accordingly.

Another way to customize weather report formats is to use visual elements such as charts, graphs, or icons to represent weather data. Visual elements can make the information more engaging and easier to interpret, especially for readers who may not be familiar with technical weather terminology. You can use Python libraries such as Matplotlib or Plotly to create these visual elements and incorporate them into your email updates.

Additionally, you can personalize weather reports by including specific recommendations or tips based on the weather conditions. For example, if you are sending weather updates to a group of outdoor enthusiasts, you may want to include suggestions for outdoor activities based on the forecast. Personalizing the content of your weather reports can make them more relevant and valuable to your audience.

In conclusion, customizing weather report formats can enhance the effectiveness of your automated email updates and provide valuable information to your audience. By including specific details, using visual elements, and personalizing the content, you can create weather reports that are informative, engaging, and tailored to the needs of your readers. Experiment with different formatting options and see what works best for your business and audience.

Chapter 9: Automating Weekly Project Status Reports

Creating Project Status Reports with Python

In the fast-paced world of business, keeping stakeholders informed about the progress of projects is crucial for success. With Python, businesses can automate the process of creating and sending project status reports, saving valuable time and resources. This subchapter will explore how Python can be used to streamline the creation and distribution of project status reports, making the task more efficient and effective for all businesses.

One popular use case for Python in business is automating the sending of weekly project status reports to project managers. By writing a Python script that pulls data from project management tools and generates a comprehensive report, businesses can ensure that project managers are always up to date on the status of their projects. This not only saves time for project managers, but also ensures that important information is never overlooked.

Another common application of Python in business is automating the sending of monthly progress reports to team members. By creating a Python script that gathers data from various sources and compiles it into a comprehensive report, businesses can keep team members informed about the progress of their projects and highlight any areas that may need attention. This automation not only ensures that team members are always informed, but also helps to improve communication and collaboration within the team.

Python can also be used to automate the sending of personalized birthday emails to clients. By writing a Python script that pulls client data and sends out personalized birthday greetings, businesses can show their clients that they care about them on a personal level. This not only strengthens client relationships, but also helps to build loyalty and trust with clients.

Additionally, Python can be used to automate the sending of monthly financial reports to stakeholders. By creating a Python script that pulls financial data from various sources and generates a detailed report, businesses can keep stakeholders informed about the financial health of the company. This automation not only saves time for stakeholders, but also ensures that they have all the information they need to make informed decisions about the business.

Overall, using Python to automate the creation and sending of project status reports can greatly benefit businesses of all sizes. By streamlining the process and ensuring that stakeholders are always informed, businesses can improve communication, save time, and make better decisions for the future. With the power of Python, businesses can take their reporting processes to the next level and achieve greater efficiency and effectiveness in their operations.

Sending Reports to Project Managers via Email

One of the most valuable uses of email automation in business is the ability to send important reports to project managers on a regular basis. By using Python scripts, businesses can streamline this process and ensure that project managers are always kept up to date on the progress of various projects.

To begin this process, businesses can utilize the smtplib and email libraries in Python to create a script that will automatically generate and send weekly project status reports to project managers. These reports can include key metrics, milestones achieved, and any potential roadblocks that need to be addressed.

In addition to weekly project status reports, businesses can also set up Python scripts to send automated reminders for upcoming deadlines to project managers. By automating this process, project managers can stay on top of important dates and ensure that projects are completed on time.

Furthermore, businesses can use Python to automate the sending of monthly progress reports to team members. These reports can highlight individual and team accomplishments, as well as outline goals for the upcoming month. By automating this process, businesses can save time and ensure that team members are always informed and motivated.

Overall, utilizing Python for email automation in sending reports to project managers is a valuable tool for all businesses. By automating the process of generating and sending reports, businesses can save time, improve communication, and ensure that project managers are always informed and up to date on the progress of various projects.

Tracking Project Progress and Milestones

Tracking project progress and milestones is crucial for the success of any business. By monitoring and analyzing the progress of projects, businesses can ensure that they are on track to meet their goals and deadlines. In this subchapter, we will discuss how to effectively track project progress and milestones using Python automation techniques.

One way to track project progress is to automate the sending of weekly project status reports to project managers. By using Python scripts with the smtplib and email libraries, businesses can set up automated emails that provide detailed updates on the status of each project. These reports can include information on key milestones, progress made, and any potential roadblocks that need to be addressed.

In addition to weekly project status reports, businesses can also use Python automation to send monthly progress reports to team members. These reports can provide a comprehensive overview of the progress made on each project, as well as any upcoming milestones or deadlines that need to be met. By automating the sending of these reports, businesses can ensure that team members are kept informed and motivated to work towards their goals.

Another useful application of Python automation in tracking project progress is sending automated reminders for upcoming deadlines. By building a script that sends reminders to team members as deadlines approach, businesses can ensure that projects stay on track and are completed on time. This can help to prevent any last-minute rushes or delays that could impact the overall success of a project.

Finally, businesses can use Python automation to send personalized birthday emails to clients and automated event reminders to attendees. By building scripts that send these emails automatically, businesses can ensure that their clients and event attendees feel valued and appreciated. This can help to strengthen relationships with clients and ensure that events run smoothly and are well-attended.

Overall, tracking project progress and milestones using Python automation can help businesses to stay organized, informed, and on track to meet their goals. By setting up automated processes for sending project status reports, progress updates, reminders, and personalized emails, businesses can save time and resources while ensuring the success of their projects.

Chapter 10: Sending Event Reminders to Attendees

Building a Python Script for Event Reminders

In the world of business, efficiency is key. One way to streamline your communication processes is by automating email reminders and notifications. In this subchapter, we will explore how to build a Python script for event reminders, which can be useful for businesses in a variety of niches.

Automating event reminders is a great way to ensure that attendees do not forget about important meetings, conferences, or other gatherings. By using Python, a powerful and versatile programming language, you can create a script that will automatically send out reminders to all participants at specified intervals before the event.

To begin building your Python script for event reminders, you will first need to set up the necessary libraries. The smtplib and email libraries are commonly used for sending emails programmatically in Python. By importing these libraries into your script, you will have access to all the tools you need to send automated reminders.

Next, you will need to define the details of the event, such as the date, time, location, and any other relevant information. This data can be stored in variables within your script, making it easy to customize the content of each reminder email based on the specifics of the event.

Once you have set up the libraries and defined the event details, you can then write the code to send the reminder emails. This may involve creating a loop that iterates through a list of attendees and sends a personalized email to each individual. By including dynamic content such as the event name and date in the email body, you can ensure that each reminder is tailored to the recipient.

In conclusion, building a Python script for event reminders is a valuable tool for businesses looking to improve their communication processes. By automating the sending of reminders to attendees, you can ensure that important events are not overlooked and that everyone is well-informed and prepared. With the right approach and a solid understanding of Python programming, you can create a script that will save you time and effort while enhancing the efficiency of your business operations.

Customizing Event Reminder Templates

In the world of business, staying organized and keeping communication lines open is crucial. One way to streamline these processes is by automating email reminders and notifications using Python scripts. By customizing event reminder templates, businesses can ensure that important deadlines, events, and updates are never missed.

To begin customizing event reminder templates, businesses can start by creating a Python script that pulls in relevant information such as event dates, times, and details. By using the smtplib and email libraries, businesses can easily set up automated email reminders to send at specified intervals before an event.

For example, businesses can use Python to send personalized birthday emails to clients, automated reminders for upcoming deadlines, or event reminders to attendees. By setting up these reminders in advance, businesses can save time and ensure that important information is communicated effectively.

Additionally, businesses can use Python to automate the sending of monthly progress reports to team members, financial reports to stakeholders, or project status reports to project managers. By customizing the content and formatting of these reports, businesses can ensure that recipients receive the information they need in a clear and concise manner.

Overall, customizing event reminder templates using Python can greatly improve efficiency and communication within a business. By automating these processes, businesses can focus on other important tasks while ensuring that key information is delivered in a timely manner. Whether it's sending daily sales reports, monthly progress reports, or event reminders, Python scripts can help businesses stay organized and keep stakeholders informed.

Automating Reminder Delivery for Events

In today's fast-paced business environment, staying organized and keeping track of important events can be a challenge. Automating reminder delivery for events can help businesses ensure that employees, clients, and stakeholders are informed and prepared for upcoming deadlines, meetings, or milestones. By leveraging the power of Python scripting, businesses can streamline their communication processes and improve efficiency.

One key application of automating reminder delivery for events is in sending personalized birthday emails to clients. By creating a Python script that pulls client birthday information from a database and automatically sends out birthday greetings, businesses can show their clients that they care and strengthen customer relationships. This simple gesture can go a long way in building loyalty and trust with clients.

Another important use case for automating reminder delivery is in sending out event reminders to attendees. Whether it's a team meeting, conference, or networking event, keeping attendees informed and engaged is crucial for the success of the event. By setting up a Python script that sends out automated event reminders with all the necessary details, businesses can ensure that attendees show up on time and are well-prepared.

Additionally, businesses can use Python scripting to automate the sending of monthly progress reports to team members. By creating a script that pulls data from project management tools and generates customized progress reports, businesses can keep their team members informed about project milestones, deadlines, and accomplishments. This not only saves time for team members but also ensures that everyone is on the same page and working towards common goals.

Moreover, automating reminder delivery for events can also be applied to sending out monthly financial reports to stakeholders. By building a Python script that pulls financial data from accounting software and automatically sends out reports to stakeholders, businesses can improve transparency and accountability. This automated process ensures that stakeholders are kept informed about the financial health of the business and can make informed decisions based on real-time data.

In conclusion, automating reminder delivery for events using Python scripting can help businesses improve communication, save time, and enhance productivity. By leveraging the capabilities of Python libraries such as smtplib and email, businesses can create customized scripts to send out automated reminders for birthdays, events, progress reports, financial reports, and more. With the right tools and strategies in place, businesses can streamline their communication processes and focus on driving growth and success in today's competitive business landscape.

Chapter 11: Setting Up Notifications for Website Uptime Monitoring

Monitoring Website Uptime with Python

In today's digital age, having a reliable and functional website is crucial for businesses of all sizes. Monitoring website uptime is essential to ensure that your online presence is always available to customers. With Python, you can easily automate the process of monitoring your website's uptime and receive notifications in case of any downtime.

To start monitoring your website uptime with Python, you will need to first install the necessary libraries. The requests library can be used to send HTTP requests to your website and check its status code. Additionally, the smtplib library can be used to send email notifications in case of any downtime. By combining these libraries, you can create a script that regularly checks your website's uptime and sends alerts when needed.

Creating a Python script for website uptime monitoring is a straightforward process. You can use the requests library to send a GET request to your website and check the status code. If the status code indicates that the website is down, you can use the smtplib library to send an email notification to yourself or your team members. By scheduling this script to run at regular intervals, you can ensure that you are always aware of any downtime issues.

Automating website uptime monitoring with Python can save businesses valuable time and resources. Instead of manually checking your website's uptime, you can rely on a Python script to do the work for you. This allows you to focus on other important tasks while ensuring that your online presence is always up and running smoothly.

Overall, monitoring website uptime with Python is a valuable tool for businesses looking to maintain a reliable online presence. By automating the process of checking for downtime, you can ensure that your website is always available to customers. Whether you are a small startup or a large corporation, using Python for website uptime monitoring can help streamline your operations and improve your overall online performance.

Sending Notifications for Website Downtime via Email

In the world of business, it is crucial to stay on top of any issues that may arise with your website. One of the most effective ways to do this is by setting up automated notifications for website downtime via email. By utilizing Python, businesses can easily create a script that will send alerts to the appropriate individuals when the website goes offline.

Automating the process of sending notifications for website downtime via email can save businesses valuable time and resources. With Python's smtplib and email libraries, setting up this automation is straightforward and efficient. By creating a script that continuously monitors the website's uptime, businesses can ensure that they are immediately alerted to any potential issues.

Not only does automating website downtime notifications help businesses react quickly to technical issues, but it also demonstrates a commitment to providing a seamless online experience for customers. By proactively addressing downtime, businesses can maintain their reputation and customer satisfaction levels. Additionally, by using Python to automate this process, businesses can streamline their operations and focus on other critical tasks.

By setting up automated notifications for website downtime via email, businesses can stay ahead of potential problems and ensure that their online presence remains strong. Whether it's a small glitch or a major outage, having a system in place to alert key stakeholders can prevent significant disruptions to operations. With Python's capabilities, businesses can easily create a reliable and efficient solution for monitoring website uptime and addressing any issues promptly.

In conclusion, leveraging Python for automating notifications for website downtime via email is a valuable tool for all businesses. By setting up this automation, businesses can proactively address technical issues, maintain customer satisfaction, and streamline their operations. With Python's versatility and ease of use, businesses can create a script that effectively monitors website uptime and sends alerts when needed. By investing in this automation, businesses can ensure that their online presence remains strong and reliable.

Customizing Monitoring Settings for Website Performance

In order to effectively monitor the performance of your website, it is essential to customize your monitoring settings to ensure that you receive timely and accurate updates on any issues that may arise. By customizing your monitoring settings, you can tailor the alerts and notifications you receive to suit your specific needs and preferences.

One way to customize your monitoring settings for website performance is to set up automated reminders for upcoming deadlines through email. By using Python to create a script that sends automated reminders to team members about upcoming deadlines, you can ensure that important tasks are completed on time and that your website continues to function smoothly.

Additionally, you can use Python to automate the sending of monthly progress reports to team members. By setting up a script that automatically generates and sends progress reports via email, you can keep your team informed about the status of various projects and ensure that everyone is on the same page when it comes to achieving your business goals.

Another way to customize your monitoring settings for website performance is to set up automated notifications for website uptime monitoring. By using Python to create a script that monitors your website's uptime and sends notifications via email if any downtime is detected, you can quickly address any issues that may impact the performance of your website and ensure that your online presence remains strong.

Overall, by customizing your monitoring settings for website performance using Python, you can streamline your monitoring processes, improve communication with team members, and ensure that your website operates at peak efficiency. With the right tools and techniques in place, you can effectively monitor and manage the performance of your website to support the success of your business.

Chapter 12: Conclusion and Next Steps

Recap of Email Automation Strategies with Python

In this subchapter, we will recap some of the key email automation strategies that can be implemented using Python. These strategies are essential for all businesses looking to streamline their communication processes and increase efficiency in delivering important information to stakeholders.

One of the most common uses of Python for email automation is in automating weekly email newsletters using the smtplib and email libraries. By creating a Python script, businesses can schedule and send out newsletters to subscribers without manual intervention, saving time and ensuring consistency in communication.

Another valuable application of Python in email automation is in creating scripts to send automated daily sales reports via email. By automating this process, businesses can ensure that sales teams have access to up-to-date information on their performance, enabling them to make data-driven decisions to drive revenue.

Python can also be used to automate the sending of monthly progress reports to team members. By setting up a Python script to generate and send these reports at regular intervals, businesses can keep their teams informed and aligned on the progress of projects and goals.

Additionally, Python can be leveraged to build scripts that send personalized birthday emails to clients. By automating this process, businesses can show appreciation to clients on their special day, enhancing customer relationships and loyalty.

Lastly, businesses can use Python to automate the sending of monthly financial reports to stakeholders. By setting up a Python script to generate and distribute these reports via email, businesses can ensure that stakeholders have timely access to critical financial information for decision-making purposes.

Overall, these email automation strategies with Python offer a range of benefits for busines across different niches, from improving communication processes to enhanci stomer relationships and increasing operational efficiency. By implementing these strategies, businesses can streamline their email communication and ensure that important information reaches the right audience at the right time.

Tips for Enhancing Email Automation Efforts

In today's fast-paced business world, email automation has become an essential tool for staying connected with customers, team members, and stakeholders. By using Python scripts,

businesses can streamline their communication processes and ensure that important information is delivered promptly and efficiently. Here are some tips for enhancing your email automation efforts and maximizing the benefits of using Python for weekly newsletters, reports, and reminders.

First and foremost, it's important to familiarize yourself with the smtplib and email libraries in Python. These libraries provide the necessary tools and functions for sending emails programmatically, allowing you to customize and automate your email communication. By mastering these libraries, you can create scripts that send automated daily sales reports, monthly progress updates, personalized birthday emails, and more to your target audience.

Another key tip for enhancing your email automation efforts is to schedule and organize your email campaigns effectively. By setting up a Python script to send weekly project status reports, monthly financial statements, or event reminders at specific times and dates, you can ensure that your messages are delivered when they are most relevant and impactful. This level of automation not only saves time and effort but also helps you maintain consistency and reliability in your communication efforts.

Additionally, consider leveraging Python's capabilities for data analysis and visualization to enhance the content of your automated emails. By incorporating charts, graphs, and other visual elements into your reports and newsletters, you can present complex information in a clear and engaging manner. This not only makes your emails more informative and visually appealing but also helps your recipients better understand and interpret the data you're presenting.

Furthermore, don't overlook the importance of personalization in your automated email campaigns. By building scripts that send personalized birthday greetings to clients or customized event reminders to attendees, you can create a more personalized and engaging experience for your recipients. This level of personalization not only strengthens your relationships with customers and stakeholders but also increases the effectiveness and impact of your email communication.

Lastly, remember to continuously monitor and optimize your email automation efforts to ensure their effectiveness and relevance. By setting up scripts to send automated reminders for upcoming deadlines, notifications for website uptime monitoring, or daily weather updates, you can proactively address issues and keep your audience informed and engaged. By staying proactive and responsive in your email automation efforts, you can maximize the benefits of using Python for your business's communication needs.

Resources for Further Learning and Development

In order to continue expanding your knowledge and skills in efficient email automation using Python, there are numerous resources available for further learning and development. Whether you are looking to automate weekly email newsletters, daily sales reports, monthly progress reports, personalized birthday emails, financial reports, reminders for upcoming deadlines, daily weather updates, project status reports, event reminders, or website uptime monitoring notifications, there are resources tailored to meet your specific needs.

One valuable resource for further learning and development in Python email automation is online tutorials and courses. Websites such as Coursera, Udemy, and Codecademy offer a variety of courses on Python programming and email automation techniques. These courses often provide step-by-step instructions, practical exercises, and real-world examples to help you deepen your understanding and proficiency in using Python for email automation in business.

Additionally, books and e-books dedicated to Python programming and email automation can serve as valuable resources for further learning and development. Titles such as "Automate the Boring Stuff with Python" by Al Sweigart and "Python Automation Cookbook" by Jaime Buelta provide in-depth explanations, code samples, and best practices for automating various email tasks using Python. These resources can help you enhance your skills and stay current with the latest trends and techniques in Python email automation.

Furthermore, online forums and communities dedicated to Python programming and email automation are excellent resources for connecting with like-minded professionals, sharing knowledge and experiences, and seeking advice and guidance on specific challenges or projects. Websites such as Stack Overflow, Reddit, and Python.org offer forums, discussion boards, and Q&A sections where you can interact with experts, ask questions, and learn from others in the field of Python email automation.

Lastly, attending workshops, conferences, and networking events focused on Python programming and email automation can provide valuable opportunities for hands-on learning, collaboration, and professional growth. Events such as PyCon, EuroPython, and DjangoCon bring together industry experts, thought leaders, and practitioners to discuss the latest trends, tools, and techniques in Python programming and email automation. By participating in these events, you can gain new insights, exchange ideas, and build relationships with fellow professionals in the field.

Title: Python: Empowering the World through Simplicity and Versatility Introduction Python, a high-level programming language, has revolutionized the world of technology and innovation.

Since its inception in the late 1980s, Python has grown into one of the most popular and versatile programming languages, making significant contributions across various domains. This report explores how Python has made everything easier for the world by its simplicity, versatility, and widespread adoption.

Simplicity and Readability One of Python's greatest strengths is its simplicity and readability. Its clean and concise syntax, resembling human language, makes it easy for beginners to learn and understand.

Python's minimalist design philosophy, often referred to as "Pythonic," emphasizes simplicity and clarity, enabling developers to write elegant and maintainable code. Example: python Copy code # Python code to calculate the factorial of a number def factorial(n): if n == 0: return 1 else: return n * factorial(n-1) Versatility and Scalability

Python's versatility enables it to be used across a wide range of applications, from web development and data analysis to artificial intelligence and scientific computing. Its extensive standard library and rich ecosystem of third-party packages provide developers with powerful tools and frameworks to tackle diverse challenges.

Example: Web Development: Django and Flask are popular Python frameworks for building dynamic web applications. Data Science: Libraries like NumPy, pandas, and scikit-learn empower data scientists to analyze and visualize data efficiently. Artificial Intelligence: TensorFlow and PyTorch are widely used for developing machine learning and deep learning models.

Scripting and Automation: Python's scripting capabilities make it ideal for automating repetitive tasks and system administration. Widespread Adoption Python's popularity and community support have led to its widespread adoption across industries and academia.

It is the preferred choice for many organizations, including tech giants like Google, Facebook, and Netflix, as well as startups and educational institutions worldwide. The vibrant Python community, comprising developers, enthusiasts, and educators, fosters collaboration, knowledge-sharing, and continuous improvement.

Example: Python in Education: Python's simplicity and versatility make it an ideal programming language for teaching computer science and coding skills to students of all ages.

Open Source Projects: Python's open-source nature encourages innovation and fosters the development of countless libraries, frameworks, and tools that benefit the global community.

Conclusion Python has undoubtedly made everything easier for the world by democratizing access to technology, empowering developers to build robust and scalable solutions, and fostering innovation and collaboration across industries.

Its simplicity, versatility, and widespread adoption continue to drive its success and relevance in an increasingly digital and interconnected world. As Python evolves and adapts to emerging trends and challenges, its impact on society and the future of technology remains profound and enduring.

Python is a general-purpose, high-level programming language that has gained immense popularity in recent years. It is known for its simplicity, versatility, and ease of use, making it a top choice for developers of all levels.

In this book, we will explore the various features and capabilities of Python, from its simple syntax to its powerful libraries and frameworks. We will delve into the world of web development, data science, machine learning, and artificial intelligence, showcasing how Python can be used to create a wide range of applications.

Whether you are a beginner looking to learn the basics of programming or an experienced developer looking to expand your skill set, this book has something for everyone. We will provide step-by-step tutorials, real-world examples, and hands-on exercises to help you master Python and unleash its full potential.

By the end of this book, you will have a solid understanding of Python and its applications, allowing you to tackle any programming challenge with confidence. So, grab your copy and embark on a journey into the world of Python programming today!

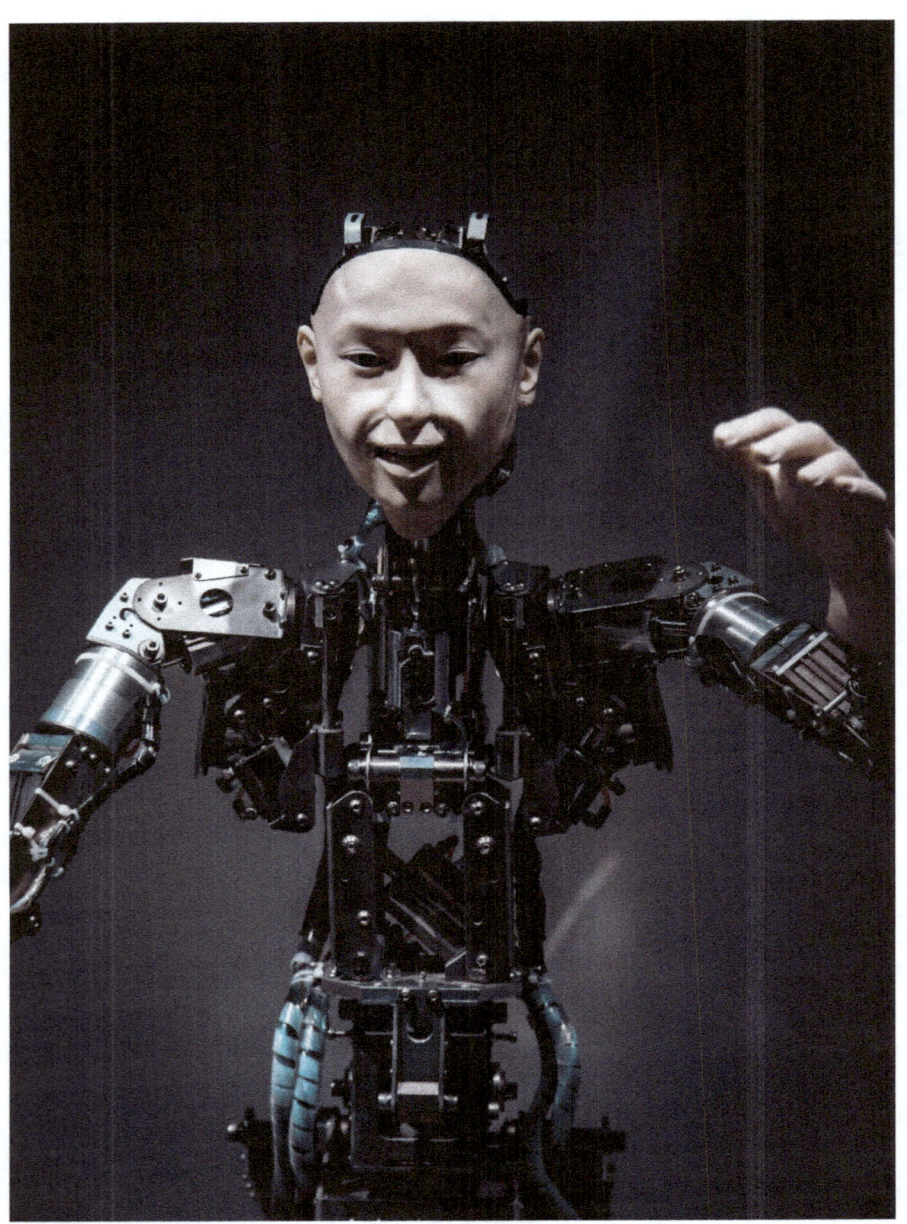

Python is an example of a general-purpose, high-level programming language . It is used for a wide variety of applications, including web development, data science , machine learning , and artificial intelligence.

Python is known for its simple, easy-to-read syntax, which makes it a popular choice for beginners and experienced programmers alike. Here are some of the key features of Python: Easy to learn: Python has a simple, easy-to-read syntax that makes it a popular choice for beginners.

Powerful: Python is a powerful language that can be used for a wide variety of tasks, from web development to data science. Versatile: Python is a versatile language that can be used on a variety of platforms, including Windows, Mac, and Linux. Free and open source: Python is free and open source software, which means that it is freely available to use and distribute.

Python is a popular choice for a variety of applications, including: Web development: Python is a popular choice for web development, thanks to its powerful frameworks like Django and Flask. Data science: Python is a popular choice for data science, thanks to its powerful libraries like NumPy and Pandas.

Machine learning: Python is a popular choice for machine learning, thanks to its powerful libraries like TensorFlow and PyTorch. Artificial intelligence: Python is a popular choice for artificial intelligence, thanks to its powerful libraries like Keras and scikit-learn. Python is a powerful and versatile language that can be used for a wide variety of tasks. It is a popular choice for beginners and experienced programmers alike.

Title: Mastering Selection Statements in Python

Chapter 1: Introduction to Selection Statements In Python programming, selection statements are essential constructs that allow you to control the flow of your program based on certain conditions. The most commonly used selection statement in Python is the if statement, which enables you to execute specific blocks of code based on whether a given condition is true or false.

Chapter 2: The if Statement The if statement is the cornerstone of selection in Python. It evaluates a condition and executes a block of code if the condition is true. Otherwise, it skips the block of code and moves on to the next statement. python Copy code age = int(input("How old are you?")) if age >= 18: print("You are an adult.") else: print("You are a minor.")

Chapter 3: The if-else Statement The if-else statement extends the functionality of the if statement by allowing you to specify an alternative block of code to execute if the condition is false. python Copy code num = int(input("Enter a number: ")) if num % 2 == 0: print("The number is even.") else: print("The number is odd.")

Chapter 4: The elif Statement In situations where you have multiple conditions to evaluate, you can use the elif statement, short for "else if". This statement allows you to check additional conditions if the preceding ones are false. python Copy code score = int(input("Enter your exam score: ")) if score >= 90: print("Your grade is A.") elif score >= 80: print("Your grade is B.") elif score >= 70: print("Your grade is C.") elif score >= 60: print("Your grade is D.") else: print("Your grade is F.")

Chapter 5: Nested Selection Statements Selection statements can be nested within each other to handle more complex decision-making scenarios.

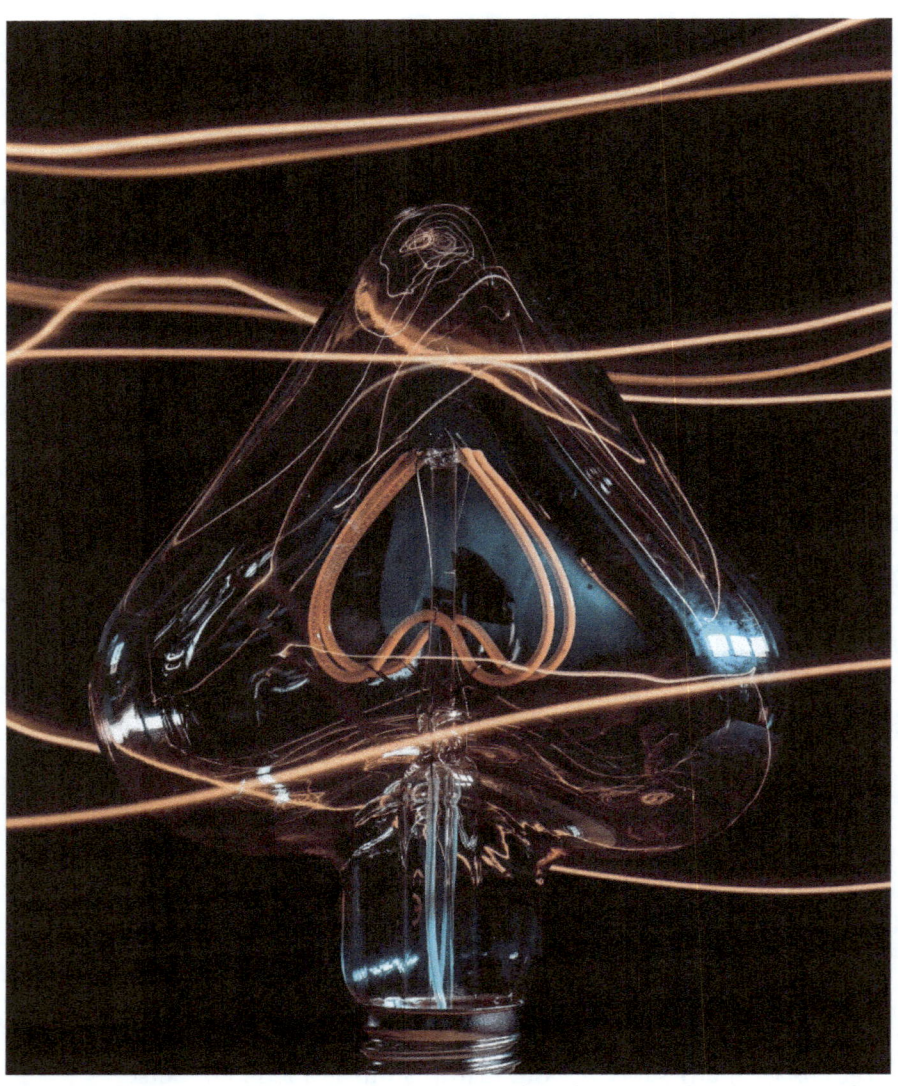

This allows you to evaluate multiple conditions and execute different blocks of code accordingly. python Copy code x = int(input("Enter a number: ")) if x > 0: if x % 2 == 0: print("The number is positive and even.") else: print("The number is positive and odd.")

elif x == 0: print("The number is zero.") else: print **("The number is negative.")**

Chapter 6: Conclusion Selection statements are fundamental to programming in Python, enabling you to create dynamic and responsive code that adapts to different scenarios. By mastering the if, if-else, elif, and nested selection statements, you gain the ability to control the behavior of your programs with precision and clarity.

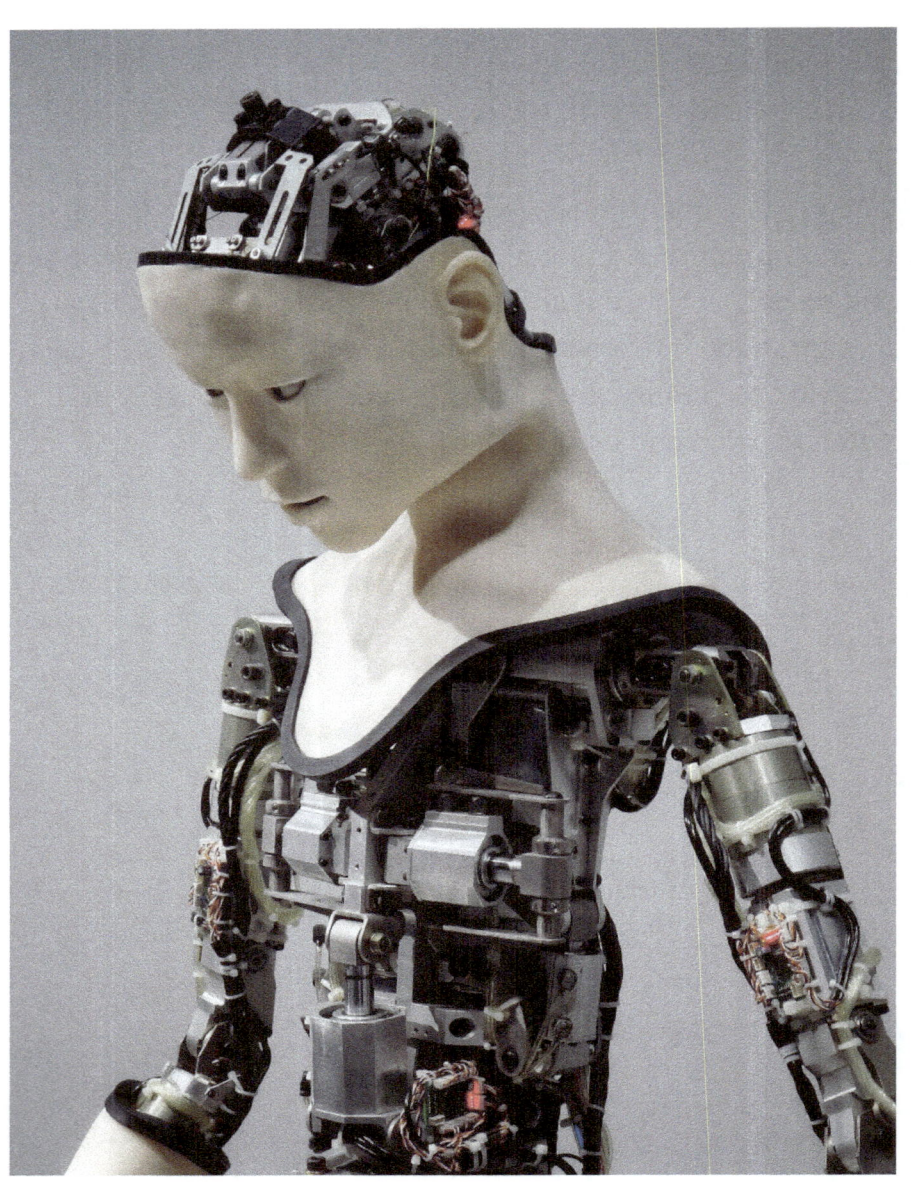

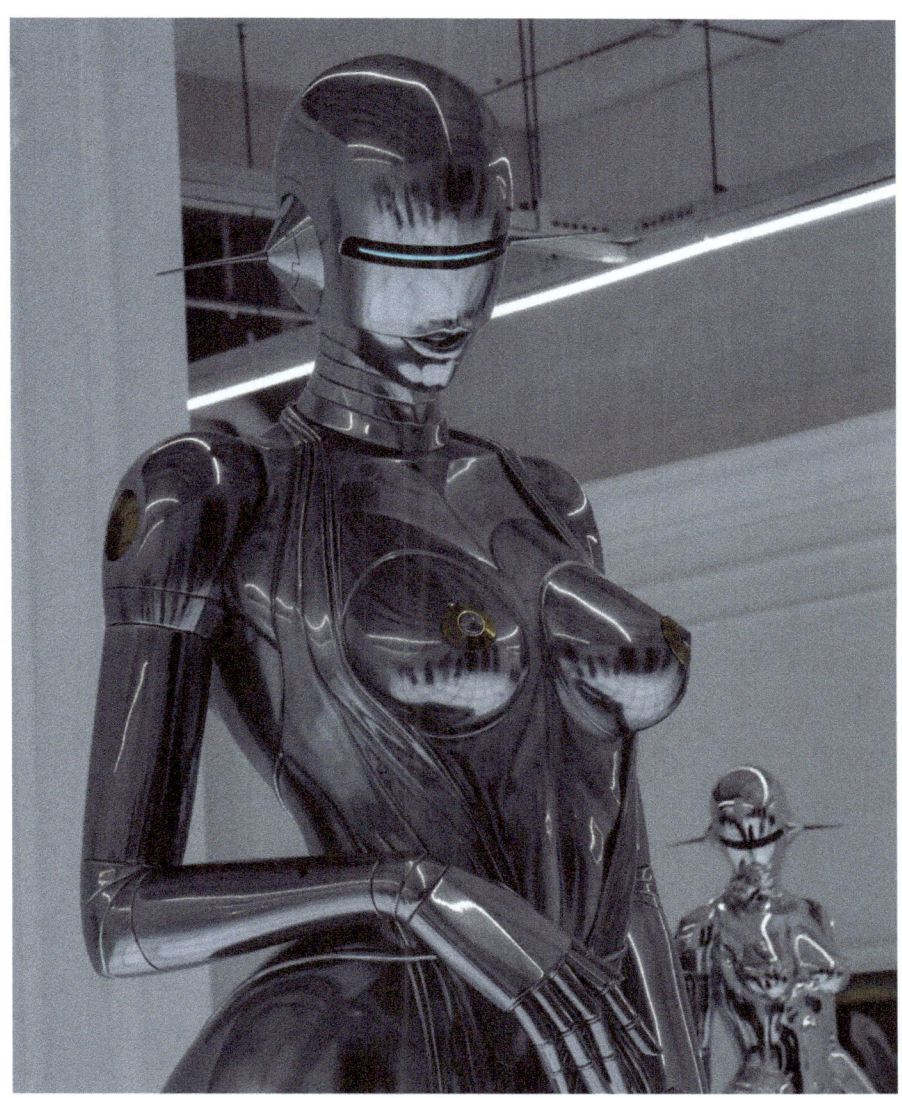

Title: Enhancing Python with Artificial Intelligence:
A Path to Simplicity and Efficiency Introduction Artificial Intelligence **(AI) and Python, two powerful technological forces, have converged to shape the future of innovation and problem-solving.**

Now this part of my book explores the symbiotic relationship between AI and Python, illustrating how AI techniques can enhance Python's capabilities and streamline various aspects of development, ultimately making everything easier and more efficient for programmers and users alike.

Chapter 1: The Fusion of AI and Python In this chapter, we delve into the foundational concepts of AI and Python, exploring their individual strengths and how they complement each other. We examine the role of Python as a versatile programming language and the capabilities of AI techniques such as machine learning, natural language processing, and computer vision.

Chapter 2: Automating Python Development AI-driven automation holds immense potential for streamlining Python development workflows. We discuss how AI-powered tools can automate tasks such as code generation, debugging, and optimization, freeing developers from mundane chores and enabling them to focus on higher-level problem-solving.

Chapter 3: Enhancing Python Libraries with AI Python's extensive ecosystem of libraries and frameworks can be enriched and augmented with AI capabilities. We explore how AI techniques can enhance libraries like NumPy, pandas, and scikit-learn, enabling more intelligent data analysis, predictive modeling, and decision-making.

Chapter 4: Intelligent Code Assistance and Suggestions AI-driven code assistants and intelligent IDEs can revolutionize the way developers write and debug Python code.

We discuss how AI models trained on vast repositories of code can provide context-aware suggestions, detect errors, and offer real-time assistance, significantly improving productivity and code quality.

Chapter 5: Natural Language Processing in Python Python's simplicity and readability make it an ideal language for natural language processing (NLP) tasks. We explore how AI-powered NLP techniques can be integrated into Python applications to enable tasks such as sentiment analysis, text summarization, and language translation, opening up new possibilities for communication and interaction.

Chapter 6: Python-Powered AI Applications AI-driven applications built with Python are transforming industries and enhancing user experiences. We showcase real-world examples of Python-powered AI applications in fields such as healthcare, finance, autonomous vehicles, and entertainment, illustrating the transformative impact of AI-powered innovation.

Chapter 7: Future Directions and Challenges As AI continues to evolve, so do the opportunities and challenges for enhancing Python with AI. We discuss emerging trends such as deep learning, reinforcement learning, and AI ethics, and explore how Python can adapt to meet the evolving demands of AI-driven innovation while addressing ethical considerations and societal impacts.

Conclusion The convergence of AI and Python represents a powerful synergy that promises to revolutionize the way we develop software, analyze data, and interact with technology. By harnessing the capabilities of AI to enhance Python's simplicity, versatility, and efficiency, we pave the way for a future where programming becomes more accessible, intelligent, and impactful than ever before.

Photograph credits go out 2 Designrr https://www.designrr.io
I would like 2 acknowledge the following photographers and sources 4 their contributions of the photographs used N this book: Cover photo: and through out this book. I extends my appreciation 2 these talented photographers 4 their stunning imagery, which adds depth and visual appeal 2 this book. Note: These photographs came with the Designrr book writing and publishing program, there 4 this statement affirming that appropriate permissions and licenses have been obtained 4 the use of the photographs. Oh! By the way thanks a million Designrr!!!

www.ingramcontent.com/pod-product-compliance
Lightning Source LLC
Chambersburg PA
CBHW070350230526
45471CB00006B/2506